Cow hunters all had dogs called catch dogs that helped chase the cows from the brush. Using their mouths, they sometimes held the cows by their nostrils until the cow hunters arrived.

Cow hunters often had to drag alligators out of their watering holes. Sometimes the musk of the riled-up gator gave the water a terrible odor and it was not fit to drink.

Florida cow hunters wore wool hats, ponchos, wide pants, and boots to their knees to protect themselves from snakes and saw grass.

Three cow hunters and a dog could round up and herd five hundred cows.

Prairie in central Florida was wide open and full of grasses.

In the late 1800s, ranches and cattle brought people to central Florida. They faced range wars and cattle rustling just like ranchers in the frontier West.

# Kissimmee Pete,
## Cracker Cow Hunter

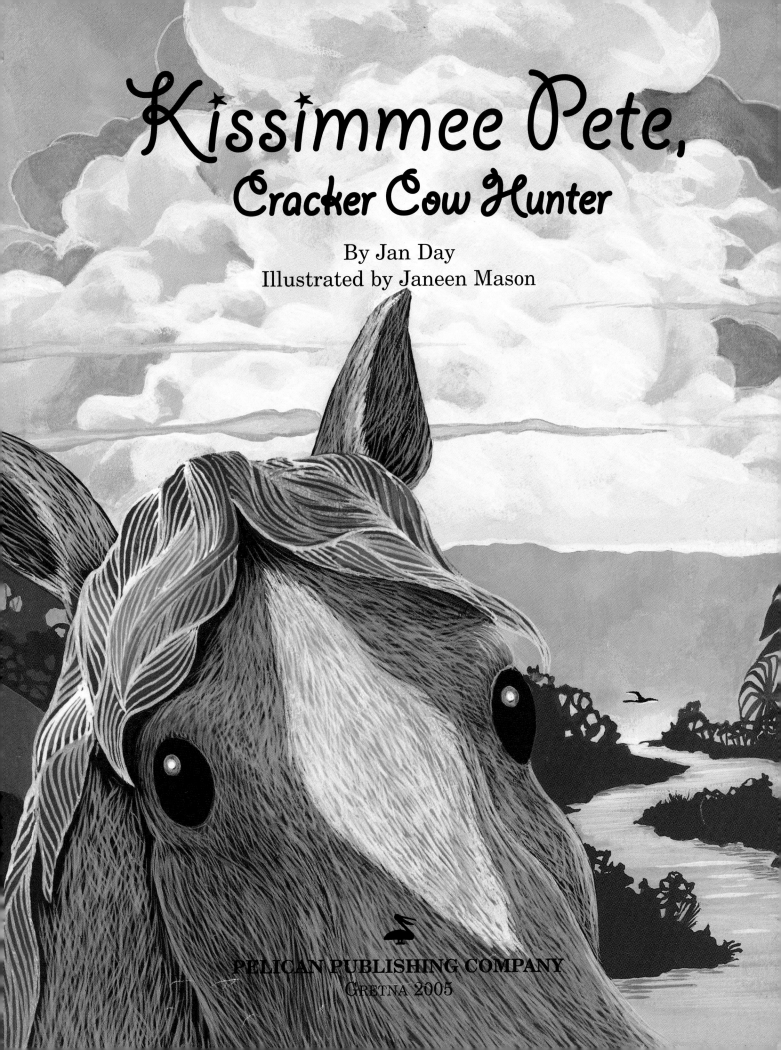

# Kissimmee Pete,
## Cracker Cow Hunter

By Jan Day

Illustrated by Janeen Mason

PELICAN PUBLISHING COMPANY

GRETNA 2005

*To Alan and Alicia with love. And many thanks to Janeen for working her magic again.—J. D.*

*To my husband, Kevin, for his unwavering encouragement. To Judge Nelson E. Bailey, the JudgeStoryTeller, for use of his endless photographic reference. And finally to Dewayne Hazelleif, the real deal when it comes to cracker cow hunters.—J. M.*

*The word "Pelican" and the depiction of a pelican are trademarks of Pelican Publishing Company, Inc., and are registered in the U.S. Patent and Trademark Office.*

**Library of Congress Cataloging-in-Publication Data**

Day, Jan, 1943-
    Kissimmee Pete, cracker cow hunter / by Jan Day ; illustrated by Janeen Mason.
        p. cm.
    Summary: Kissimmee Pete, his dog Mud, and his horse Blaze work together to gather a cow herd "as big as the sky."
    ISBN-13: 978-1-58980-325-1 (hardcover : alk. paper)
    [1. Cowboys—Fiction. 2. Florida—Fiction.]  I. Mason, Janeen I., ill. II. Title.
    PZ7.D3315Kis 2005
    [E]—dc22
                                                    2005011288

Printed in Singapore
Published by Pelican Publishing Company, Inc.
1000 Burmaster Street, Gretna, Louisiana 70053

## KISSIMMEE PETE, CRACKER COW HUNTER

One starry night when Pete the cow hunter was taking a bath, he looked up to see a bean-green cow leap over the moon and land with a flop in the middle of the Kissimmee River. No one ever knew where String Bean came from except Pete, who claimed mosquitoes flew her in from Silver Springs.

Since Pete had his speedy horse Blaze but no herd, he was mighty interested in the little critter, even if she was bean green. He pulled that cow back to shore by its tail. Now Pete had a pretty cow to be proud of. Mud, the catch dog, kept her in line.

After that, everyone called him Kissimmee Pete, the clever cow hunter, although some said he got his name 'cause the girls were always after him for a smooch.

Pete spied two wild cows hidin' in the saw palmetto. Faster than a skeeter can bite, he took off after 'em. Mud, the catch dog, ran ahead, yipping as loud as he could. When no ropin' or callin' or barkin' would get them to budge, Pete scratched his head, stamped his boot, and said, "I got me a whopper of an idea."

He made himself a fine leather whip, which he snapped above the brush. The crack of the whip scared those old knotheads right out into the open. Pete became known as a "cracker." At least that's what the folks in Florida called him: Kissimmee Pete, the clever, cracker cow hunter.

Pete, Blaze, String Bean, and Mud slept under a glittering sky. Pete bunked down on the ground with his poncho pulled over him. But when skeeters bigger than buzzards started pokin' their bones, String Bean and Blaze climbed in right next to Pete. Mud was already there. By morning, all four were a mite cranky.

During roundup, Pete rode with other cow hunters who were driving their herds to port. "This is the most dangerous job in the world," said Kissimmee Pete, the cranky, clever, cracker cow hunter, as he fought off a rattler, wolf, and panther all at the same time. Mud kept an eye on the squirrels.

One night when the boys gathered round the campfire in the middle of a hammock, they heard a ferocious noise. Kissimmee Pete, the courageous, cranky, clever, cracker cow hunter, and Mud, the catch dog, raced off to investigate.

Pete saw two bears fightin'. They pushed and shoved each other until one got so mad it chased the other right up a tree and into the clouds.

The fur began flying until one cloud grew so heavy with hair it fell to earth along with the bears. Pete thought the fuzzy cloud would make a nice blanket to keep off the bugs.

The hairless bears did, too. Pete and Mud yanked one way and the bears pulled another. Even though he was stronger, Pete let them win. "They need that blanket more than I do," said Kissimmee Pete, the tender-hearted, courageous, cranky, clever, cracker cow hunter.

Those two bears took off runnin' through the trees. You can still see wisps of fuzzy cloud caught on the low-hangin' branches. Some people who don't know the true story call it Spanish moss.

Pete went to bed, but no poncho, smudge pot, or net would keep off the skeeters. By the next morning, he wished he'd kept that blanket to hide under. Blaze was in such a bad temper due to a night of bitin' mosquitoes that he didn't feel like working at all.

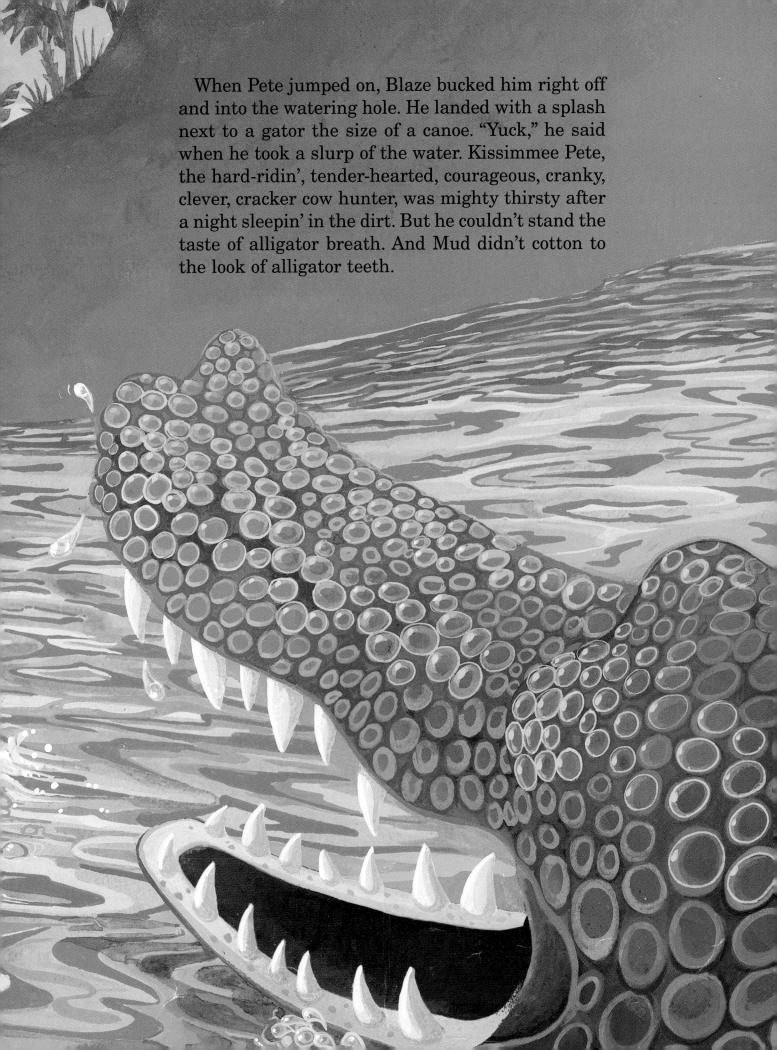

When Pete jumped on, Blaze bucked him right off and into the watering hole. He landed with a splash next to a gator the size of a canoe. "Yuck," he said when he took a slurp of the water. Kissimmee Pete, the hard-ridin', tender-hearted, courageous, cranky, clever, cracker cow hunter, was mighty thirsty after a night sleepin' in the dirt. But he couldn't stand the taste of alligator breath. And Mud didn't cotton to the look of alligator teeth.

The gator took exception to sharing his spot and chomped a hole out of Pete's pants. That was a big mistake.

Kissimmee Pete, the stinky, hard-ridin', tender-hearted, courageous, cranky, clever, cracker cow hunter, wrestled that old gator and tied him up to a tree. Then the cows came down for a drink.

Pete dried himself off with grass. Mud came out of hiding.

But the gator chewed right through the rope and plunged into the middle of the herd.

"They ain't your dinner!" Kissimmee Pete, the gator-wrestlin', stinky, hard-ridin', tender-hearted, courageous, cranky, clever, cracker cow hunter, shouted, but the cows were already blasting full speed ahead to somewhere else.

"*Stampede!*" Pete yelled.

The cow hunters chased them varmints from Lake Okeechobee to the Everglades before they caught up with them. By then, the cows were so riled up they were kicking each other and paid no mind to the cow hunters or Mud.

Then Pete and Mud crooned an old cow hunter's lament. String Bean sang a tenor moo. Blaze yodeled the chorus. The tired herd fell fast asleep. Kissimmee Pete, the velvet-voiced, gator-wrestlin', stinky, hard-ridin', tender-hearted, courageous, cranky, clever, cracker cow hunter, said it was due to their way with a song.

Just before dawn, a swarm of starvin' mosquitoes munched down on those poor critters and sucked the stuffing right out of 'em. Pete said they looked more like beef jerky than cows on the hoof. They were so flat they fit in the back of the chuck wagon. But wouldn't you know it, the rainy season had begun. Rivers rose, flowing over the prairies and lowlands.

Pete put his brains to use again. He tossed the cows right into the river, and just like a sponge, each one filled back up to its full size and took off swimming to the other side.